Follett

$ 17.95

DATE DUE			

35043210010139

921
Bez

Garty, Judy.

Jeff Bezos :
business genius of
Amazon.com

CLEAR LAKE INTERMEDIATE SCHOOL
HOUSTON, TX

1/06

Jeff Bezos
Business Genius of Amazon.com

INTERNET BIOGRAPHIES

BILL GATES
Software Genius of Microsoft
0-7660-1969-1

LARRY ELLISON
Database Genius of Oracle
0-7660-1974-8

ESTHER DYSON
Internet Visionary
0-7660-1973-X

STEVE CASE
Internet Genius of America Online
0-7660-1971-3

JEFF BEZOS
Business Genius of Amazon.com
0-7660-1972-1

STEVE JOBS
Computer Genius of Apple
0-7660-1970-5

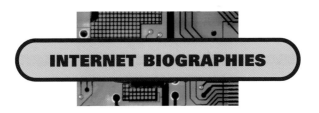

INTERNET BIOGRAPHIES

Jeff Bezos
Business Genius of Amazon.com

by Judy Garty

Enslow Publishers, Inc.

40 Industrial Road   PO Box 38
Box 398   Aldershot
Berkeley Heights, NJ 07922   Hants GU12 6BP
USA   UK

http://www.enslow.com

PRODUCED BY:
Chestnut Productions
Russell, Massachusetts

Editor and Picture Researcher: *Mary E. Hull*
Design and Production: *Lisa Hochstein*

Copyright © 2003 by Enslow Publishers, Inc.

Library of Congress Cataloging-in-Publication Data

Garty, Judy.
  Jeff Bezos : business genius of Amazon.com / by Judy Garty.
     p. cm. — (Internet biographies)
Summary: Explores the life and career of the creator of the online bookstore Amazon.com, discussing his early interest in computers, business philosophy, and plans for the future.
Includes bibliographical references and index.
  ISBN 0-7660-1972-1
  1. Bezos, Jeffrey—Juvenile literature. 2. Booksellers and bookselling—United States—Biography—Juvenile literature.
3. Amazon.com (Firm)—History—Juvenile literature. 4. Internet bookstores—United States—Juvenile literature. [1. Bezos, Jeffrey.
2. Booksellers and bookselling. 3. Businesspeople. 4. Amazon.com (Firm) 5. Internet bookstores.] I. Title. II. Series.
Z473.B47G37 2003
380.1'45002'028454678—dc21

                              2002153174
Printed in the United States of America

10 9 8 7 6 5 4 3 2 1

To our readers:
We have done our best to make sure all Internet addresses in this book were active and appropriate when we went to press. However, the author and the publisher have no control over and assume no liability for the material available on those Internet sites or on other Web sites they may link to. Any comments or suggestions can be sent by e-mail to comments@enslow.com or to the address on the back cover.

Illustration Credits: Associated Press/Wide World Photos, pp. 2, 4, 9, 12, 18, 24, 26, 34; Corbis, p. 28; Reuters, p. 39.

Cover Illustration: Associated Press/Wide World Photos

Opposite Title Page: Amazon.com founder Jeff Bezos flashes his signature smile.

CONTENTS

The Amazon company headquarters rises up from its location atop Beacon Hill in Seattle, Washington.

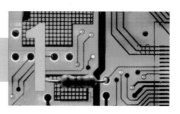

The Visionary

The garage floor of Jeff Bezos's rented home in Bellevue, Washington, was a maze of extension cords. The car-and-a-half space was crowded with computers and cabinets, heaters and halogen lights, chalkboard walls, and a desk made from a used door. Two multi-task computer servers called Sun SPARC stations were rigged to ring a bell every time any one of his five workers sold a book, and within weeks of July 16, 1995, the noise was deafening. The online bookstore Amazon.com was born—and its thirty-five year-old father, Jeff Bezos, was on his way to becoming a multi-billionaire and Internet icon.

The idea for Amazon.com, billed as the world's largest bookstore, started in 1994 when Bezos was asked to research Internet business opportunities. At the time, he was a senior vice president at D.E. Shaw, a financial company in New York. Bezos made a list of twenty possibilities, and selling books was number one. Worldwide there were 3 million books in print.

Major United States book distributors like Ingram's had used digital lists of their books since the late 1980s. Bezos thought books would sell well online, but he couldn't convince his boss of this.

So he decided to start his own online book selling business. He believed anything was possible on the World Wide Web, which was just becoming popular and growing by 2,300 percent annually. He asked himself, "When I'm eighty, am I going to regret leaving Wall Street? No. Will I regret missing the beginning of the Internet? Yes."[1] So Bezos left New York to start his own business.

Bezos had the idea and the desire, but he didn't know where or how he would begin his e-business. Unafraid, he and his new wife, Mackenzie Tuttle Bezos, packed up their apartment, took the family dog, flew to Texas to borrow a car from his dad, and told the movers to start driving west. It wasn't until the next day that Bezos would tell them exactly where.

After making another list—this time of places that might work for his business—Bezos settled on Seattle, Washington. It had many talented computer people and was close to Ingram's Oregon book distribution center, the country's largest. Usually only customers who live in the state where a business is located have to pay sales tax, so the state of Washington was a good choice for an e-business. It had a smaller population than many states, which meant the company would have fewer sales-taxed

This is what it looks like inside Amazon's Seattle warehouse during the holiday rush. The company brings in extra workers and even puts executives to work boxing and wrapping holiday orders.

customers. Seattle was also the home of Bezos's friend Nicholas Hanauer, who later invested in Amazon.com.

Not everyone believed in Bezos's idea. Bezos himself figured his business had only a 30 percent chance of success. He told would-be investors it would take a long time to make money. But over the next months, Bezos found over a dozen family members, friends, and business people who together gave $2 million to Bezos to start his company.

As his wife drove them to Seattle in a 1988 Chevy Blazer, Bezos made cell phone calls and drew up a business plan on his laptop. Before arriving in Seattle, he met three computer programmers in Santa Cruz,

California, and hired Shel Kaphan as his first employee. Bezos was looking for computer people who believed in his vision, and he looked for his workers carefully.

Building a two gigabyte database of over a million book titles meant months of work. Bezos and his crew had to design a Web site, study available software, create new software, and debug programs. Kaphan compared one of their tasks, moving book titles from a reference CD-ROM to their own database, to "emptying a swimming pool using a drinking straw."[2]

They had to decide how to handle credit cards securely, update book lists, process orders, and let people know about Amazon.com. The company's original name was Cadabra, Inc. "Cadabra" was meant to

THE MIDAS TOUCH

There's a certain Midas touch to Jeff Bezos artifacts. The used-door office desk Bezos built when he began his business raised over $30,000 for charity in 1999 at his Amazon.com auction site. The desk drew almost twice as much as a copy of *A Farewell to Arms* signed by the author, Ernest Hemingway, an autographed photo of the late President John F. Kennedy, and a prized Beanie Baby combined. Bezos's mother, Jackie, got to keep her son's handiwork, and the World Wildlife Fund got the money to help save wildlife habitat in the Amazon River Basin. Even a bathrobe Bezos had worn only once raised nearly fifty dollars.

have the magic of "Abracadabra" but it was once misheard as "cadaver," a term for a dead body. So in 1995, the name was changed to Amazon.com. Just as the Amazon River carries one-fifth of all the river water flowing into earth's oceans, and its vast basin covers an area the size of the continental United States, Bezos wanted his business to be the biggest and best.

"[Bezos] is a really young, really smart guy who had a big idea and the nerve and will to go and pull it off,"[3] said Jonathan Weber, editor-in-chief of *Industry Standard* magazine.

Bezos saw Amazon.com as a new way of life where customers could find whatever they wanted online quickly and easily. He kept improving the Web site to make it customer friendly. He wanted it to be a fun site where visitors would return again and again. When people logged on to Amazon.com, Bezos wanted them to feel at home.

Amazon Board member Patty Stonesifer said of Bezos, "I don't think he's a showman, but people are drawn to him because he seems unbelievably like a winner. And they want to help him win."[4]

Jeff Bezos has been an avid reader since childhood. As a volunteer for the Read Across American program, he read his favorite children's book, The Stinky Cheese Man, to audiences.

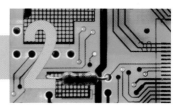

The Explorer

As a boy, Jeff Bezos was full of curiosity. He was always building and dissecting, experimenting, playing with toys and electronics, and thinking of the future. He had a pet raccoon and later a dog. He liked to spend time with his family, take photographs, read about outer space, and make plans. Thomas Edison and Walt Disney were his heroes, and he went to Disney World six times. Even though he was on the small side, he had big ideas.

Jeffrey Preston Jorgensen was born January 12, 1964, in New Mexico. He didn't know his real father and was adopted at age four when his mom, Jacklyn "Jackie" Gise married Miguel "Mike" Bezos. The family moved three times, and Bezos spent many summers with his grandpa. It didn't bother him to learn he was adopted, but he cried at age ten when he found out he had to wear glasses.

Bezos learned a lot from his family. His mother was happy to let her son explore, and she fed his curiosity. His adoptive father, a Cuban refugee who learned English at age seventeen, had worked himself through school and become a successful executive with the Exxon oil company. His grandfather, Preston Gise, worked on space technology for the United States Department of Defense. Gise was later named by Congress to manage the Atomic Energy Commission's western region and supervise its 26,000 employees.

When Bezos was little, he kept his mother busy. At age three he had a crib, but he wanted a grown-up bed. So he tried to make himself one by taking the crib apart with a screwdriver! He would get so involved in an activity that the only way his Montessori school teachers could move him to a new one was to carry him, chair and all.

At River Oaks Elementary School in Houston, Texas, Bezos loved a motorized toy whose mirrors let him see into infinity. He wanted his own Infinity Cube, but his mom didn't want to pay twenty dollars to buy one. So Bezos figured out what he needed, bought the parts, and made one himself.

When he was in fourth grade, Bezos spent hours playing a primitive Star Trek game. He knew how to use the time-share computer that linked his school and a Houston business better than his teachers. Bezos joined a youth football league. The coach made him defensive captain because he could remember the plays and positions of all ten players.

When Jeff was in the sixth grade, the Bezos family moved to Florida. "There was always something going on in our garage," said his mother. "His projects became more complex with age, but unfortunately the garage never got any bigger."[1]

Some of Jeff's projects worked and some didn't. He liked building models and making things. He set up a warning buzzer, like a burglar alarm, to let him know when his brother Mark or sister Christina was in his room. He would later help Mark and Christina build wonderful science projects like seismographs. Using an umbrella and some aluminum foil, Bezos once made a solar microwave. He tried, unsuccessfully, to turn a Hoover vacuum cleaner into a hovercraft.

From ages four through sixteen, Bezos spent summers on his grandpa's ranch in Texas. Retired, Preston Gise encouraged Bezos's curiosity and interest in science. Bezos learned to fix tractors and windmills, ride horses, drive a car, lay pipe, and repair pumps, as well as to brand and vaccinate cattle. He built a crane and a barn, took cattle to auction, and repaired a giant bulldozer. During the hottest part of the day, he went inside to watch television.

Jackie Bezos thought ranch work taught her son to rely on himself and make decisions. She said, "One of the things [Jeff] learned is that there really aren't any problems without solutions. Obstacles are only obstacles if you think they're obstacles. Otherwise, they're opportunities."[2]

When Bezos was at Palmetto High School, he enjoyed science, avoided drugs and alcohol, and told his classmates he would become the valedictorian of their 1982 class—which he did. He got good grades, worked at McDonald's, joined the National Honor Society, and was a National Merit Scholar finalist. He graduated at the top of a class of 680 students and won several awards in math and science. He dreamed of space hotels and orbiting amusement parks and thought he might grow up to be an astronaut or physicist. As a prize for a paper he wrote on zero gravity and the common horsefly, he attended the NASA Marshall Space Flight Center in Huntsville, Alabama.

Jeff also liked to laugh and have a good time, and he had a knack for details. When a good friend, Ursula Werner, turned eighteen, Bezos created a road rally/treasure hunt for her. He planted clues at a Miami bank, by a railroad track, and in the restroom of a Home Depot store.

BEZOS'S FIRST BUSINESS

DREAM Institute was the summer camp that Bezos set up with his friend Ursula Werner in the summer of 1982. Books Bezos and Werner wanted their campers to read included: *Black Beauty, David Copperfield, Dune, Gulliver's Travels, The Lord of the Rings, The Once and Future King, Stranger in a Strange Land, Treasure Island, Watership Down,* and the plays *Our Town* and *The Matchmaker.*

In the summer of 1982, Bezos and Werner ran a summer camp called DREAM (Directed REAsoning Methods) Institute. Five neighborhood kids from grades four, five, and six signed up for the two-week, three-hour sessions about science and literature, black holes and photography, fossil fuels and space travel. Using his Apple II computer and a dot-matrix printer, Bezos made a flyer advertising DREAM Institute's new approach to old ideas. Bezos and Werner each earned about $300. It was Bezos's first original business venture.

As a college student, Jeff Bezos enjoyed looking for ways that computers could be used to improve science and business practices.

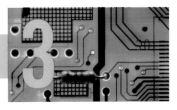

The Mastermind

Bezos went to Princeton University in New Jersey from 1982 to 1986. He was president of his fraternity and a member of Students for the Exploration and Development of Space. Even though he was among the top twenty-five students in the honors physics program, he decided there were students more talented in that field than he was, so he switched to electrical engineering and computer science, which he loved. He built a special computer for measuring tiny DNA detail, and he graduated with honors.

Like most college kids, Jeff worked in between his studies. When his father was transferred to Norway, Bezos worked in Stavanger, Norway, as a programmer/analyst for Exxon. Using an IBM 4341 computer, he came up with an easy way to figure out oil royalties. One summer he worked in San Jose, California, for IBM's Santa Teresa Research Labs. He finished in three days a project that was expected to take four weeks.

Already Bezos was figuring out how to make computers work faster and more simply.

After graduating from Princeton, he was offered many jobs. He joined Fitel, a high-tech company in New York, where he supervised global networks and improved rules that let computers communicate with each other. Graciella Chichilnisky, Bezos's boss at Fitel, saw his business talent. "He will anticipate the changes," she said. "I bet on Jeff Bezos's brain."[1]

In 1988, Bezos worked for Bankers Trust Company, becoming their youngest vice president, and he earned a Masters degree in business administration from Harvard University. While at Bankers Trust, he headed a programming department that created a communications network for clients who shared about $250 billion in assets. The way Bezos was using personal computers was new. He replaced hard copy information with an easy-access software program. The program was used in the offices of more than one hundred Fortune 500 companies. This change allowed bank clients to check on their own invest-ments, using a computer.

When Bezos was twenty-six years old, he met Halsey Minor, a Merrill Lynch analyst. Minor had an idea for a computer system that would send out com-pany information using graphics, animation, and hyperlinks. Backed by Merrill Lynch, the two men signed a contract to develop an intranet of personal news faxes for finance professionals. An intranet is an internal communications system that allows users to share information over a computer. But after a few weeks, the New York company changed its mind and dropped its funding for the project.

Bezos was meeting people, growing his reputation, and finding new ways to do things. In 1990, he joined a Wall Street firm, D. E. Shaw, which had been started by a computer science professor from Stanford University. The company was cutting edge; it looked

ALWAYS LOOKING FOR SOMETHING NEW

Jeff Bezos has always been fascinated with new ideas, and he finds them everywhere. After visiting a self-service pineapple stand in Hawaii, where an on-your-honor cashbox replaced a salesperson, Bezos got the idea for the Amazon Honor System. The Amazon Honor System made it possible (and easy) for Web users to donate money to support their favorite Web sites.

In 1997, Bezos ran a contest inviting customers to write sentences for a murder mystery started and ended by author John Updike. About 400,000 people responded and six earned a $1,000 prize. When, contrary to company policy, e-mail became backlogged at Amazon.com, Bezos sponsored a customer service contest and paid $200 to employees who answered 1,000 emails in 48 hours. And when an inventor named Dean Kamen announced he was working on a secret, high-tech transportation device, Bezos signed up to sell the machines at Amazon.com, even before the details of the scooter-like device were known.

for talent and encouraged innovation. In 1992, Bezos became the company's youngest senior vice president. It was also at D.E. Shaw that he met, fell in love with, and—in 1993—married Mackenzie Tuttle, a researcher and writer.

After reading a report that said Web usage was expected to grow 2,300 percent annually, Bezos began researching which products would sell well online. He decided that books, computer hardware, computer software, CDs, and videos would sell well. Bezos had done his homework. Nearly a decade later, books and computer hardware were still the top products in online retail sales, according to the United States Census Bureau, which keeps track of e-business statistics. By 1994, Bezos was confident that his idea of selling books over the Internet was a good one.

AMAZON.COM STATISTICS

	Net Sales	Total Operating Expense	Net Loss
1996	$15.7 million	$ 9.9 million	$ 6.2 million
1997	$ 148 million	$61.4 million	$ 31 million
1998	$ 610 million	$ 243 million	$125 million
1999	$ 1.64 billion	$ 896 million	$720 million
2000	$ 2.76 billion	$ 1.51 billion	$1.41 billion
2001	$ 3.12 billion	$ 1.21 billion	$567 million

Source: Amazon.com

By the time Bezos left New York to begin his own business, he had several advantages. He knew a lot about computers. He had built programs for many different tasks and was excited about the computer's business future. His travels had helped him understand the world market and given him professional contacts. People who had worked with Bezos knew he was smart, creative, and dedicated.

Bezos's parents supported his new idea. "When he called and said he wanted to sell books on the Internet, we said, 'The Internet? What's that?'" said his dad.[2]

"We talked about it for two minutes," said his mom. "We didn't invest in Amazon; we invested in Jeff."[3] Bezos's parents gave him $300,000—most of their retirement money—because they believed in him.

Bezos had his idea for Amazon.com at just the right time. Even though the Internet began in the early 1960s and the Web was launched in 1991, it wasn't known to most people until 1993. As the cost

JEFF BEZO'S NET WORTH

Year	Wealth
1999	5.74 billion dollars
2000	4.05 billion dollars
2001	1.23 billion dollars

Source: *Fortune Magazine*

The shelves of Amazon's distribution center in Seattle are full of books. One of the biggest challenges Amazon faced was how to get books to customers fast. Today, Amazon's books can often be purchased, wrapped, and delivered within twenty-four hours.

of computers dropped, more people could afford to have them. As technology improved, people saw how many things computers could do. Eventually, computers became as common as televisions. People began to use the Internet to shop, just as they had once used catalogs.

There were many things Bezos had to do to make his online business dream come true. He had to learn about book selling and figure out the best way to find books and deliver them to customers quickly. He had to design a Web site and decide how to organize information about books, orders, shipping choices, and business records.

Bezos was sure he had a good idea. He knew a computer could store countless more book titles than a bookstore could hold books. He knew his customers would be pleased if he could deliver orders quickly and easily, and he wanted to make his store friendly enough that people would want to come back.

"Bezos is such a visionary. He's changing the world, making history," said Joe Galli, former Amazon president, who described Bezos as a fabulous mentor. "To sit at the table with Jeff Bezos and learn about the Internet is incredible."[4]

Jeff Bezos holds a Pokemon doll as he talks about Amazon's intention to build itself into an online superstore. Bezos wanted Amazon to sell everything from books and music to videos, toys, and hardware.

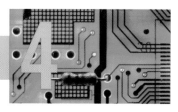

The Pioneer

B ezos wasn't afraid to work hard and take risks some people might disagree with. For him the Internet was like the Wild West before the Gold Rush. He wanted to be the first settler in this exciting new territory. The same excitement and interest that drew him to space and the Infinity Cube pushed him to build a new way of shopping.

Instead of the free parking, escalators, and glass display cases of store buildings, Bezos offered free browsing, easy access, and clear information on Amazon.com's Web site. He invented one-click ordering, a fast and safe way for repeat customers to place orders. He only wanted to improve what the customer would see, so Amazon's physical workspace wasn't fancy. Company meetings were sometimes held in hallways.

In the beginning, Bezos packaged books on a cement floor with staff until early morning and then took boxes to the post office. One night he came up

Workers at Amazon's United Kingdom distribution center prepare to send out 65,000 copies of Harry Potter and the Goblet of Fire. *It was the biggest selling book in the history of online sales.*

with the idea of buying kneepads. But a co-worker had a better idea—tables. "It never occurred to me we should get packing tables!"[1] Bezos said.

From the very start, Bezos had a virtual dream that Amazon.com could carry visitors into a new kind of shopping experience. Books, including rare and out-of-print books, were the beginning of that dream. Without any advertising, in its first month Amazon sold books in all fifty states and in forty-five countries. "Within the first few days, I knew this was going to be huge," said Bezos. "It was obvious that we were onto something much bigger than we ever dared to hope."[2]

Other booksellers, both large and small, were afraid of Amazon's competition. They feared the attraction, ease, speed, and low price of ordering books through Amazon would steal their business. Publishers, however, saw the online bookseller as an ally.

Amazon got even bigger. It started to sell music in 1998, and within four months it was the number one online music seller. After that, it added video and DVD movies, toys, electronics, software, home improvement products, hardware, auctions, greeting cards, zShops, and an online flea market. Next came housewares, luxury items, cars, and local groceries.

Bezos wanted to move Amazon.com from the Biggest Bookstore to the Earth's Biggest Store. He saw Disney, FedEx, and Microsoft as role models. Knowing it had taken eleven years for the newspaper *USA Today* to make a profit, he was content to wait to make money.

By 1999, Amazon had over 3 million square feet of storage space in seven states and three countries. Delivery trucks ran from 5:30 A.M. to late afternoon. The warehouses were a well-organized system of scanners, conveyor belts, bins, color-coded lights, chutes, cubbyholes, labeling and packaging areas, and loading docks. By the year 2000, Amazon staff numbered 7,000; in 2001, Amazon had 10,000 vendors, 600,000 associates and 30 million worldwide customers.

What began by word of mouth grew into radio ads, local banners, and full-page print ads. Even though all of Amazon's products would fill more than forty New York City phone books, Bezos ran a small 2000 holiday catalog. In 2001, he test-mailed a new catalog that included tools, outdoor living items, and housewares. He started Radio Amazon to keep in touch with his staff, kept a beeper handy, and made quick, cutting-edge decisions.

To Bezos, the customer was key. He invited customers to fill out "About You" pages, write book reviews, sell books, e-mail opinions, create wish lists, and become associates. Bezos made Amazon accessible from anywhere in the United States with Palm VII devices or Internet cell phones. He updated the list of top children's books weekly, refused to sell firearms or pets, and promoted the idea "Earth Day Every Day." He offered discounts, mood matchers, gift suggestions, gift wrap, and card services. Bezos kept track of individual tastes and made sure repeat customers knew about items of interest to them. When customers looked for a book, they received information about that book as well as a list of other related titles.

"We've been saying for a long time our goal is to build a place where people can come and find . . . anything they want to buy. That's anything with a capital 'A,'" said Bezos, describing an A to Z goal on which he was willing to work for many years. "What we're trying to do is create a shopping environment that has zero risk, zero hassles, and zero products you can't find," he said.[3]

Bezos worked hard to personalize Amazon.com. "The notion is that you take customers and put them at the center of their own universe," he said.[4]

In 1999, *Time* named Bezos Person of the Year for his role in changing the way we do business. He was the fourth youngest person to receive the honor.

AMAZON.COM — A THROUGH Z

At the turn of the century, you could buy all of these things at Amazon.com:

A art supplies, amplifier **B** birdbath, boom box, board games **C** card games, calendar, compass, CDs, camera, **D** dishes, dictionary, DVDs **E** e-cards, easels **F** folding chair, flashlight, flags **G** guitar, garden gloves **H** hammock, heart muffin pan **I** ink pens **J** jewelry, jump rope **K** karaoke machine **L** lacrosse shirt, log cabin building sets **M** magnets, microphone, magnifying glass **N** Nepalese necklace **O** outdoor furniture **P** piano, perfume, power tools, **Q** quilting books **R** rocketry handbook, robotic pets, radio **S** scooter, shampoo, statues, Star Wars stuff **T** telescope, tool set, Thai weaving **U** umbrella, underwater propulsion machine **V** video games **W** wireless phone, watches, wind chimes **X** x-ing sign for ladybugs **Y** yo-yo, yoga videos **Z** zebra rug

Previous honorees included Charles Lindbergh, the first pilot to fly solo non-stop across the Atlantic Ocean. Just as Lindbergh had launched a new era in flight, Bezos had launched a new era of e-commerce. "This is an incredible and humbling honor," said Bezos. "The Internet holds the promise to improve lives and empower people. I feel very lucky to be involved in this time of rapid and amazing change."[5]

Despite its growth, Amazon.com had problems. Sales were staggering from the beginning, but covering business expenses was costly. Whatever money the company made was already spent. In its first five years of operation, the company failed to make a profit. Some shareholders grew impatient with Bezos's promises of profit. Many investors lost money. Amazon.com's first public stock shares sold at $18 per share. But by October 1, 2001, Amazon stock had hit an all-time low of $5.51. It was reported Bezos was losing money on every sale. By the end of 2001, his business was $2 billion in debt. Analysts asked Amazon's board of directors whether they planned to find someone to replace Bezos. Bezos laid off workers in 2000 and 2001, moved headquarters three times, and closed warehouses.

The future of Amazon.com was uncertain. There was a possibility it would not survive. But it was clear that Bezos himself was more than a survivor—he was a leader. He stayed committed to his vision and his customers, who came in growing numbers.

It wasn't until the end of 2001 that Amazon posted its first-ever profit. But, at a penny per share, Amazon earned a total of $5 million in the final quarter of 2001. It was great news for Amazon.com.

Despite some unfavorable news headlines, Bezos believed that the press and Wall Street had treated him fairly over the years. "For what happened at Amazon to happen, you have to get very, very lucky many times in a row, with no unlucky times," said Bezos.[6]

Bezos has a great sense of humor and enjoys clowning around with his staff and family. He is always using his wild imagination to dream up new ideas. He says he wakes up every morning thinking of ways to improve customer service.

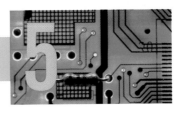

The Hurricane's Eye

Bezos lived his company's motto—"work hard, have fun, make history." He felt there was plenty of room for online competition. And he was not bothered by people who did not share his way of thinking. He tried to stay healthy, saved time for family, and laughed often. Even though his future was uncertain, Bezos kept working toward his goal. "He has the ability to really focus," said Mark Bezos, Jeff's brother. "Everyone in the family looks to Jeff for leadership."[1]

Bezos compared the Internet business to a storm. "The Internet is this big, huge hurricane," said Bezos. "The only constant in that storm is the customers."[2]

Bezos stayed close to his family. Giving his family laser tag guns and vests and wearing night vision goggles, he once battled his parents, siblings, and wife in a night game of Capture the Flag. Even a vacation grocery store run turned into a game with walkie-talkies and code names like "Ffej Sozeb"—Jeff Bezos in reverse. When his brother ran the 1999 New York Marathon, Bezos ran next to him part of the way for moral support. After his son, Preston, was born in 2000, Bezos took even greater delight in family.

He avoided distractions. He didn't pay attention to the ups and downs of Amazon's stock or sales numbers. If problems arose, he acted quickly. When a computer glitch paralyzed his business for twelve hours in 1998, Bezos gave customers a discount. Even a 6.8 Seattle earthquake in 2001 couldn't shake him—he simply moved several hundred Amazon employees outdoors to work on their laptops.

HOW BEZOS LIKED TO SPEND HIS MONEY

Bezos spent money on others and sometimes on himself. Through Amazon.com auctions, he once paid $40,000 for a skeleton of an Ice Age cave bear, $50 for a first edition of a favorite book, *Dune,* by Frank Herbert, and $11,100 for an autographed photo of Albert Einstein. Occasionally, he chartered a plane. When Shel Kaphan, Bezos's first employee, had worked at Amazon for four years, Bezos flew Kaphan's family and friends to Maui, Hawaii, for a four day celebration.

Even though he did not know how to play tennis and did not even own a pair of tennis shoes, Bezos was part of a tennis match to raise money for cancer research in 2001. That same year, when he had to layoff 1,300 workers, he put $2.5 million worth of company stock aside for them. He wanted to be a philanthropist.

"[Bezos] genuinely believes that come what may, he's going to change the fundamental equation between buyer and seller, putting more power in the consumer's hands,"[3] said *Time* columnist Joshua Quittner.

"Whether or not Amazon.com will eventually lose [under his direction] is not the main issue," wrote authors John Whitney and Tina Packer. "He has built a stupendous business, not by waiting to see what was going to happen, but by making it happen."[4]

Bezos once jumped into a rubber band war at the warehouse. In the office, he snapped photos daily, operated a remote controlled tank, and threw a toy called Slime Dog at the wall. Staff lounge foosball was one of his favorite games, and he was known to zap employees outdoors with a Super Soaker from his office window. He took his workers on a retreat, and for one company masquerade he dressed as a butler.

"There was always a certain comfort in hearing him laugh," said co-worker Scott Lipsky. "It was nice knowing that he was there and that he was as involved as you were. That's part of his being the soul of the company."[5]

Journalist Katrina Brookner once wrote, "It's almost impossible to be in the same room with Bezos and not have a good time. He's relaxed, he's funny, and he's disarmingly humble."[6]

Bezos prized every minute of the day. He liked walking six flights of stairs to his office better than riding the elevator. He took daily vitamins even when traveling, thanks to Mackenzie, who packed them into his socks. He liked short nonfat lattes, Vivaldi violin, *Battlestar Gallactica* music, science fiction books, Legos, and the biography of English explorer Sir Richard Francis Burton.

Bezos won awards and trophies. His company was on Yahoo's "What's Cool" list for ten months. Bezos was a punchline for entertainer Jay Leno and a question for the game show *Hollywood Squares*. Bezos helped talk show host Oprah Winfrey organize an auction. He was a good sport about publicity. *Time* magazine once asked him to pose in a shipping box of foam packing chips for an hour, and he came out smiling.

"We are at the tip of the iceberg," Bezos said at the turn of the twentieth century. "It's hard for people to imagine just how good e-commerce is going to be ten years from now."[7]

Bezos imagined blazing more trails in the future. He believed his company would some day make money, and he wanted to help people with his money. He pictured a time when books could be downloaded or printed on demand, one copy at a time, and read on computer screens. He expected faster computer speed, improved bandwidths, and the extinction of paper catalogs. He imagined custom-made goods and voice-activated mini-cell phones worn on the ear. He could see dinner plates that could

On The Tonight Show *with Jay Leno, Amazon CEO Jeff Bezos demonstrates an educational toy called "Gus's Guts." The doll allowed kids to view Gus's internal organs. It was available for sale at Amazon's Internet superstore.*

count calories and medicine bottles that could warn people about harmful drug interactions. He pictured fog-like flying robots the size of dust particles that could link to form solid, useable objects. He envisioned a caring community of commerce.

"For the industry as a whole, it's still day one," said Bezos, who had been fascinated with new ideas since his youth. "The alarm clock hasn't gone off yet," he said, imagining a future where people would depend on the Internet as much as they once had on cell phones. "I firmly believe this is the Kitty Hawk era of e-commerce. Charles Lindbergh hasn't even been born yet."[8]

CHRONOLOGY

1964   Jeffrey Preston Jorgensen is born in New Mexico on January 12.

1968   Jeffrey is adopted by Jackie and Mike Bezos.

1968–1980   Bezos spends his summers on Grandpa Gise's cattle ranch in Texas.

1969   Bezos moves to Florida with his family.

1982   Bezos graduates from high school at the top of his class and enters Princeton University.

1984   Bezos works as a programmer/analyst in Norway.

1985   Bezos modifies computer programs at an IBM Research Lab.

1986   After graduating from Princeton with honors, Bezos goes to work for Fitel.

1988   Bezos earns his MBA degree from Harvard University and joins the Bankers Trust Company.

1990–1994   Bezos works for D.E. Shaw & Co.

1993   Jeff Bezos and Mackenzie Tuttle are married.

1994   Bezos founds Amazon.com.

1995   Amazon.com is launched on the Web.

1997   Amazon.com becomes the largest online seller of music.

1998   Amazon.com becomes the number one Internet video retailer.

1999   Bezos is named *Time* magazine's Person of the Year.

2000   A son, Preston Bezos, is born.

2001   Amazon sales reach $3.12 billion.

2002   Amazon reports its first-ever profit, for the fourth quarter of the fiscal year 2001.

CHAPTER NOTES

CHAPTER ONE. The Visionary

1. Chip Bayers, "The Inner Bezos," *Wired,* Vol. 7.03, March 1999, p. 173.

2. Robert Spector, *Amazon.com: Get Big Fast* (New York: HarperBusiness, 2000), p. 53.

3. Helen Jung, "Amazon's Bezos Is the Internet's Ultimate Cult Figure," *Seattle Times,* Sept. 19, 1999, <http://archives.seattletimes .nwsource.com/cgi-bin/texis.cgi/web/vortex/display?slug=bezo&date =19990919&query=Amazon%27s+Bezos> (March 18, 2002).

4. Bayers, p. 186.

CHAPTER TWO. The Explorer

1. Helen Jung, "Amazon's Bezos Is the Internet's Ultimate Cult Figure," *Seattle Times,* Sept. 19, 1999, <http://archives.seattletimes.nwsource.com/cgi-bin/texis.cgi/web/vortex/display?slug=bezo&date=19990919&query=Amazon%27s+Bezos> (March 18, 2002).

2. Robert Spector, *Amazon.com: Get Big Fast* (New York: HarperBusiness, 2000), p. 5.

CHAPTER THREE. The Mastermind

1. Robert Spector, *Amazon.com: Get Big Fast* (New York: HarperBusiness, 2000), p. xxii.

2. "Amazon's Source," *TIMEasia,* Vol. 154, No. 25, December 27, 1999, <http://www.time.com/time/asia/magazine/99/1227/cover3.html> (March 18, 2002).

3. Ibid.

4. Katrina Brooker, "Amazon vs. Everybody," *Fortune,* November 8, 1999, p. 126.

CHAPTER FOUR. The Pioneer

1. Jeff Bezos, *Audible.com: Industry Innovators: Vol. 1*, 18:15. (Four hour, forty minute audio download available for cost through Amazon.com).

2. Amazon's Source, *TIMEasia,* Vol. 154, No. 25, Dec. 27, 1999, <http://www.time.com/time/asia/magazine/99/1227/cover3.html> (March 18, 2002).

3. Helen Jung, "Amazon.com Opens Site to Other Merchants," *Seattle Times,* Technology section, September 29, 1999, <http://archives.seattletimes .nwsource.com/cgi-bin/texis.cgi/web/vortex/display?slug=amaz&date =19990929&query=Amazon.com> (March 18, 2002).

4. Katrina Brookner, "Amazon vs. Everybody," *Fortune,* Vol. 140, No. 9, p. 126.

5. Reuters, "Man of the Year: Jeffrey Bezos," December 20, 1999, <http://www.wired.com/news/business/0%2C33176%2C00.html> (March 18, 2002).

6. "Quick Tour: Why Amazon Succeeds," *Time.com,* December 27, 1999, <http://www.time.com/time/poy/whysucceeds.html> (March 18, 2002).

CHAPTER FIVE. The Hurricane's Eye

1. Robert Spector, *Amazon.com: Get Big Fast* (New York: HarperBusiness, 2000), p. 127.

2. Ibid.

3. James Kelly, "That Man in the Cardboard Box," *Time.com,* December 27, 1999, Vol. 154, No. 26 Special, <http://www.time.com/magazine/contents> (March 18, 2002).

4. Cecil Johnson, "Shakespeare's Link to the Corporate Arena," *Seattle Times,* Business & Technology, July 31, 2000, <http://archives.seattletimes .nwsource.com/cgi-bin/texis.cgi/web/vortex/display?slug=book31&date =20000731&query=Shakespeare%27s+Link> (March 18, 2002).

5. Robert Spector, *Amazon.com: Get Big Fast* (New York: HarperBusiness, 2000), p. 184.

6. Kristina Brooker, "Amazon vs. Everybody," *Fortune,* Vol. 140, No. 9, November 8, 1999, p. 123.

7. Pete Henig and Nicole Sperling, "The Fantasy World of Jeff Bezos," *Red Herring Magazine,* August 15, 2000, http://www.redherring.com/mag/issue83/mag-bezos-83.html> (March 18, 2002).

8. Jennifer Darwin, "Amazon.com's Bezos: Digital Age Just Beginning to Reveal Its Winners, Losers," *Houston Business Journal,* September 11, 2000, <http://http://www.houston.bizjournals.com/houston/search.html> (March 18, 2002).

GLOSSARY

animation—Moving pictures.

associates—Customers linked to Amazon who earn referral fees.

Amazon honor system—A way for Amazon customers to give money to their favorite Web sites through Amazon.com.

bandwidth—The capacity of a cable or communication channel to carry data.

CD-ROM—A format for storing data on CDs. The term stands for "Compact Disc Read-Only Memory."

database—A large amount of information that serves as the basis of a Web site and which visitors to that site can examine at their leisure.

e-business—A business that is based on the Internet.

e-commerce—Business that takes place over the Internet.

entrepreneur—A risk-taker who starts a new business.

function—Something a computer can do.

graphics—Pictures and icons, as opposed to text.

hyperlinks—Highlighted words on which a computer user can click to go to other related pages.

Internet—The system of worldwide connected computer networks, of which the World Wide Web is a part.

intranet—An internal communications system for a group like a school or a business through which members can access information that pertains to them.

Kittyhawk—A town in North Carolina where, in December 1903, brothers Orville and Wilbur Wright claimed the world's first successful airplane flight.

Lindbergh, Charles—An American pilot (1902-1974), Lindbergh was an international hero at age twenty-five when he became the first aviator to fly solo non-stop across the Atlantic Ocean.

Montessori School—A hands-on method of teaching in which children are encouraged to explore their interests.

philanthropist—One who promotes goodwill to others, usually through monetary gifts.

seismograph—A record of vibrations within the earth.

software—Instructions that tell a computer how to perform tasks.

valedictorian—A top student who gives a graduation speech.

Web site—A location on the World Wide Web.

World Wide Web—An internet service that organizes information using a wide variety of linked documents.

zero gravity—A state of weightlessness.

zShops—An opportunity for retailers to link to Amazon.com and sell their goods; zShops participants open accounts, pay seller fees, and can provide photographs and descriptions of their goods.

FURTHER READING

Brackett, Virginia. *Latinos in the Limelight.* Philadelphia: Chelsea House Publishers, 2001.

Claybourne, Anna. *The Usborne Computer Dictionary for Beginners.* London, England: Usborne Publishing Ltd., 1995.

Cooper, Gail & Garry. *New Virtual Field Trips.* Englewood, Colorado: Libraries Unlimited, Inc./ Division Teacher Ideas Press, 2001.

Kalbag, Asha. *World Wide Web for Beginners.* London, England: Usborne Publishing Ltd., 1997

Kazunas, Charnan & Tom. *The Internet for Kids.* Danbury, Connecticut: Children's Press, 1997.

Sherman, Josepha. *Jeff Bezos: King of Amazon.* Brookfield, Connecticut: Twenty-First Century Books, 2001.

Spencer, Donald. *Great Men and Women of Computing.* Ormand Beach, Florida: Camelot Publishing Company, 1996.

INTERNET ADDRESSES

The official Amazon.com Web site.
http://www.amazon.com

Facts about Jeff Bezos.
http://www.thestandard.com/people/profile/0,1923,1327,00.html

A *BusinessWeek* interview with Jeff Bezos.
http://www.businessweek.com/1999/99_22/b3631011.htm

INDEX